The Epiphanies

of Prayer Book

Reverend Don W. Moses

ISBN-13:
978-1984371768

ISBN-10:
1984371762

Rev. Don W. Moses

INTRODUCTION

This book: The Epiphanies of Prayer is a compilations of stories, designed and cloaked in parables as art imitating life given to me through my prayer life when I talked to the Lord about issues or situations or problem that I had to deal with.

They are designed as coping mechanisms to insure that whatever we faced in life, through prayer, God HAS THE ANSWER. And if we but ask Him... He will give us what we need and sometimes even more so that we can handle it knowing He cares.

Most of them were given to me through meditations to teach me how conduct myself as I listen to the Lord speak to my heart where or when He chose to speak back.

This process will insolate you.......away from human resolves and re-direct your thinking to the revelations He will inspire and also create a co-dependency on His wisdom. Which is where He intends to get us involved in on a personal level.

It is my sincere hope that these epiphanies will shed light on some of life's most common yet perplexing problems while giving us a deeper and more meaningful impression of what one of God's main objectives for mankind is.

The ability to willfully talk to Him not just by falling down our knees but speaking to Him telepathically, mentally, anywhere, at any time while waiting on Him to speak back to us with enlightenments and those enlightenments are what I call: "The Epiphanies of Prayer."

Enjoy and God Bless You.

Don W. Moses

ACKNOWLEDGEMENTS

As before in my first book there so many people who are indirectly responsible for how the good things in my life have come about. First there is the Lord Jesus who inspires me through my thought processes. He makes me realize that there is a reality in a prayerful relationship that He wants to make all of us trust as the permanent resolve to all of life's issues that we are confronted with.

Secondly my sister Linda and her good friend Latina Sheard both are relentlessly in assuring that the process goes forward no matter what comes my way or mistakes I personally make trying to learn how to make things happen. Reverend(s) Jenkins, Willingham. The late Rev(s).Johnson & Dobbins. Rev. B. Alexander and Darlene Moses who were so tactful in helping me understand the art of the editing process. All have helped me so much with their expertise and encouragements.

But my wife Linda has always been the strongest influence. Who for 47 years through almost every conceivable set of circumstances stood by me when everyone didn't understand the callings on my life. It is my prayer that God blesses her efforts in life as much as she has blessed me. Thank you baby.

And may God Bless the names and influences of any person I failed to mention who know you are a part of this process...Thank you one and all...

Sincerely Rev. Don W. Moses

Table of Contents

ACKNOWLEDGEMENTS ix

A Picture Says: 1

The Pearls Before the Swine...3

Caught In the Rib-Tide 5

Running on A Busted Play..7

Deductive Rationale..9

In Search of Bobby Fisher 11

The Clubs That We Get Hit With...13

The Art of Shadow Boxing 15

Why....The Stress-Test? 17

God Won't Put You on Speaker Phone 19

Under the Black-Light 21

I Know It Was The Blood..23

The Danger of A Misdiagnosis 25

The Psychology of Spite...27

Friends Have Friends 29

Stuck In a Holding Pattern 31

The House Always Wins 33

What Do You Do...When The Joke's On You?...........35

Something for Nothing...38

Kaleidoscope 40

I'm In Here Too..42

A Copy ...From The Master-Copy...............................44

The Reading of The Will 46

Trippin' 48

Who Wins...50

LONG 52

Salvation...54

The One's I Get Wrong 56

Stuck In A Chicken Coop..58

I Had a Stunt-Double 61

The Hostage 63

A Snake Under a Rock 66

Explaining and Complaining 68

Camouflage 70

You Still Got It 72

The Path of Least Resistance 74

Manipulation 76

12 Years A Slave 79

About The Author 82

A Picture Says:

Was having a conversation with a friend who had asked me a question, which was based on some information we had previously shared.

Once I explained to him what I saw in the picture he mentally painted for me, then compared it to his, from my point of view, the difference in what we saw was as different as night and day. He couldn't understand how we saw the same picture so contrastingly different YET BEAUTIFUL...He admired my perspective more than his own and though it flattered me to hear the accolades he heaped on me, I had to tell him the truth.

That being, the only difference in what he saw and what I saw was:(the differences in our ages) and experiences

But I assured him that he was no different from me or worse or lesser than me. He was just YOUNGER. I told him this: A Picture Says...etc. a thousand words. But how is that possible when we are looking at the same thing? What makes a picture we both see look so differently when we both (SEE THE SAME PICTURE?)

Four things come into play immediately.1 The angle in which you view it. 2.The distance or closeness to or away from what he or she is viewing. 3. One's height. And lastly 4. The number of times one views the picture. Let me clarify it a bit more. 1. The position of what is viewed. 2. How familiar you are with it. 3. Your level of maturity. 4. Consistency or how often you view it.

The same is true with our prayer life and scripture reading. The more we do both, the more these things automatically come into play. It's God's way of causing us to see Him through the lenses of growth. See the more we pray, we simply approach God or what He is trying to show us from the different angles, frequency of relationship to Him, levels of maturity...and routine.

I was once told: "You Can Not Get Better At What You Do Not Practice" It's called: Development!. Jesus ,gets excited when we have an appetite for it because it helps us to see more clearly and leaves us with not enough words to describe His Glory. That is called: The Worship Experience and it is through that experience, we honor God, The Father which leaves us again speechless. Holding in our hearts a picture of Him as Lord and Savior. How He wants to be seen by us and for us to get to know Him personally and to know exactly about Him what: "A Picture Says"!!!! in describing Him. God is Awesome and it shows Him where we truly stand and (That is called): Growing In Grace
!!! 2 Cor.12:1-4, 1Cor.13:4-12...1 Cor.2:4-11,2 Pet.3:10-17.

The Pearls Before the Swine

Based on a true story: In the early farming days on a rural back woods farm in Lonoke County, Arkansas. A well-known southern farmer came up missing and had not been seen or heard from in several days. He was a well-liked, kind hearted quiet man, loved by the locals in the area. A search went out to look for him. Everyone who knew him wanted to know what happened since he lived alone on the farm. They searched the local creeks, rivers, woods, with no success. They were about to give up and return to the farm but when they got there, they decided to give it a thorough last look which ended at his hog pin and there his body was found partially eaten leaving nearly no remains, only parts of his overalls which were left mostly intact. He had been eaten by the swine.

Though it was too early in those days and before the autopsy process had been discovered the locals felt he possibly had a heart attack and fell in too helpless to remove himself while>>>>"FEEDING THEM".<<<< Don't forget that part and they ate his remains, leaving nearly nothing. We risk so much being helpful at times, not being aware of or underestimating the nature of those around us. They may not VALUE THE EXTENT of what we can share and then in our weakest moments TURN ON US NEVER understanding WE WERE TRYING TO FEED THEM SOMETHING TO NURTURE THEM because they need it. Wisdom is fast teaching me to be more selective about what I share as well as with whom I share what WITH. It came from a Bible verse I received through prayer about why what I shared and it backfired, so I through the medium of prayer asked God WHY? How do things we share confiding in those we care about get twisted? Then He reminded me of this story and said write it.!! It will help someone to confide in ME more and not in man who may not VALUE what you share and may take it wrong. Prayer and totally trusting God above people will keep you and give you better discretion about what to share and who to share it with so you will not feed things of value to the wrong people.

While giving away :Your Pearls, Your Gems, Your Diamonds, Your Jewels: unbeknownst to you those who like swine who have no sense of their value nor you...So keep your pearls confidential, as to not allow them to become "The Pearls Before The Swine!" Matthew 7:6-8; Psalm 118:5-8. G.I.G.A.T.T.

Caught In the Rib-Tide

A young life guard working the beach in Miami, sitting in his life guard's chair high above the beach and was just relaxing listening to a local radio station when all of a sudden a loud cry went out from the shore-line about a swimmer who had gotten: Caught In The Rib-Tide. A series of waves that tend to trap swimmers who are caught in their currents which prevent them from reaching the shore.

Everyone rushed to the tower where he was to beg him to go out there and save the guy. So he first pulled out his binoculars, spotted the struggling man, then slowly dismounted his chair and casually WALKED to the edge of the water, with a life preserver attached to him on a cord, stuck his feet in the water, then began to swim to the seemingly DROWNING SWIMMER.

Everybody on the beach were now becoming angry at him (THOUGH HE SAVED HIM) and revived him before the paramedics rescue squad got there, but there went a protest out about his skills by the people who saw it all, so they took him to court to sue him and have him dismissed from his job. At the hearing prior to a trial, the judge asked him a series of questions concerning the event finally he asked him: After all these things witnesses have said about you, what do you have to say for yourself and is all of it true?

He replied: "It's true your honor but they left out the most important part." See your honor I only weigh 175lbs.The drowning man, 275lbs. Do the math. "I am trained to save all my strength to return to shore alive and WITH THE APPARENT VICTIM. If I hadn't waited until the CIRCUMSTANCES subdued him, neither one of us would have made it back alive. So in order to save my strength AND HIM, I stayed close enough to him to save him....and FAR ENOUGH AWAY to let nature take it's course

The judge ruled in the life-guard's favor and said: "Cased Dismissed"!!!!

Sometimes God's like in Peter's case, in St. Mt.14:29-32 when he was walking on the sea, allows us to go through struggles He could save us from at any time, but SINKING IS NECESSARY just to hear us like Peter say: Lord, SAVE ME!!!

It insures our need to be redeemed from what we're caught up in. The Rib-Tide of what SURROUNDS us. However, God, unlike the life guard will never be overtaken no matter how many of us are drowning at the same time. He can save us all at once or individually. He did that at the Cross when He said: "Father Forgive Them. For They Know Not What They Do." Then interceded in PRAYER for us sort of like that life guard when we get "Caught In The Rib-Tide" Of life St. Lk.23:34.

<u>Running on A Busted Play</u>

After every conceivable method was used to stop number 24 from scoring, he scored anyway. The championship game was of two NFL teams thought to be evenly matched, but things came down to the running backs on both squads...with a slight advantage going to number 24. Why, because every known method to stop him was put into place by every team in the league. Year after year the opposing teams studied game film of him, his stature common among all other running backs in the league...and guess what? They won again, and he was the league's star player.

When interviewing his coach the media wanted to know out of all the teams they had played for years how number 24 always scored against every team and won for them. How did he do it they wondered? What was his secret? So, the coach said, "Since he retires this year, I will tell you how he does it. Every team has caused him setbacks due to injuries, fumbles, false starts, etc. See he is not any different from any other back...EXCEPT,he has the unique ability to know how to do what no other back does better! He knows how to take advantage of 'busted plays.'!!! They, the opposition are so busy studying him, they overlook two important factors about him: (1) His knowledge of the game (2) They are so afraid of his ability to score they fail to value WHAT HE CARRIES and ALL HE NEEDS IS A BUSTED

PLAY because it frees him to work against what is expected of him BY THE OPPOSITION. This is all he needs to fuel what is in him that cannot be taught. His INSTINCT—IT'S WHAT HE CARRIES; IT IS WHAT THEY ARE AFRAID OF. So, they try to hurt him. They try to hurt him so badly they inspire his real ability. Their inner hatred of him. He wins every time while "RUNNING ON A BUSTED PLAY!" The unpredictable. My point is simple: Prayer is the football we carry against our opposition. Life's problems are the Satanic influened predictables meant to cause us to fall, be wounded, quit, or feel overtaken.

They never count on us scoring anyway. God equipped us with a special tool when He gave us that. It will always let us score no matter what or who or how many adversities that confront us. We need that unpredictability to make us instinctively run to the only opening we have available to us. The throne "Running on A Busted Play!" Psalm 35 !

Deductive Rationale

My mentor, was a psychology major in college who was also a minister, taught me a lot ...like: How to interpret body posture, it's language, verbal errors which disclose hidden truths, how to read letters and see what people really mean when they talk to me ...by what they omit. What their eyes say, how they position themselves physically to get what they want. How simple is simple? It's so simple in fact, that if you studied it long enough, you can really be good at it.

The process of "Deductive Rationale". Doctors, detectives, lawyers, scientist, mathematicians, nuclear physicist, chemist, and forensics all use it. It's what we all become and what we are as people simply because we understand how to over-look the obvious. That is what Deductive Rationale IS. Nothing more that the process of elimination. That being: That, that is not, only leaves that THAT IS! We do it without thinking reading between the lines of things (so to speak) and seeing what's not there that IS hidden. Thus, discovering what it is people looking for answers find because of this principle. So if you want to find out what something IS, deduct ALL THAT IT IS ...NOT! Then what remains is
WHAT SOMETHING REALLY IS. EVEN WHEN YOU CAN'T DESCRIBE IT! Life has it's way of steering us to discovery things because of this principle.

To get to my point, when we have tried every human source to find cures, remedies, answers, through the process of elimination, in a gesture by most of us, we throw up our hands and lift our heads to the sky then we say: GOD IS HEAVEN ONLY KNOWS. Why do we say that? Because we've reasoned away every distraction from the answer yet UNWITTINGLY WE ARE >>PRAYING<<!!!! How about that? When all else has failed, JESUS IS THE ANSWER to: "Deductive Rationale".

That is where He was trying to get us to conclude all the time. I was sinking deep in sin. Far from the peaceful shore. Very deeply stained within. Sinking to rise no more. But the Master of the sea, heard my despairing cry. From the waters lifted me. Now safe am i. Love lifted me. Love lifted me. When NOTHING else could help, Love lifted me. God's Love. At least that's my "Deductive Rationale" of it. Eccl.3:9-14, Lk.15:11-24.

In Search of Bobby Fisher

Bobby Fisher. Probably one of the greatest chess players of all time. Most people who have ever played chess would most likely agree with me on this and most likely cannot name another chess players period, though chess is a very popular game around the world. A game that requires one's ultimate concentration, attention and the unique ability to anticipate the next move(s) of your opponent and having the right chess men in play yourself to counter any opposition they may pose.

No easy feat when you are playing the best players in the entire world. Tennis players do it all the time on the tennis court whenever they deliberately place a shot that is thought to be indefensible, a shot or play their opponent cannot respond to, to possibly defeat them.

Bobby Fisher was so good at it, he could leave an opponent sitting for hours even days during a match just trying to figure a move to counter the dilemma they, by playing him found themselves faced with.

What made him so good? First, he knew the basic fundamentals of the game. Secondly, he knew the basic counter moves, but thirdly and probably the best thing he had going for himself was he could make basic moves that would demand his opponent counter with basic moves that would eliminate their strongest chess pieces OFF THE CHESS BOARD BY HIM!

Thereby he gained the advantage long before the game had ended but get this part, he did this often, and he did this even before the game BEGAN and never started that same way with different players and that prompted any players who considered themselves a Chess Masters to: SEEK HIM OUT and try to beat him which only a hand full of them ever did but never with any regularity.

Bobby however, after gaining great notoriety became a hermit moving out of the United States and lived in obscurity until he later died but the challenge he left as his legacy was his ability to: STAY AHEAD OF THE GAME but ours is the game of life and we have a master who unlike Bobby Fisher HAS NEVER BEEN DEFEATED. And He challenges us LIKE Bobby Fisher and wants us to SEEK HIM OUT. His name is JESUS! We do it on the Chess Board of PRAYER in the game of life. He's way ahead of the game of life but will teach us the best moves to lock the board on our biggest opponent Satan. AND CHESS-MATE HIM.

When we do, we discover how much ahead of the game He is before we begin. In a prayer, the writer of the Psalms said in one of them: "Teach me oh Lord The Way Of Thy Statues, And I shall keep it unto the end"! Ps.119:33-42 the word of God and the request for the knowledge of it through prayer concludes with us winning and out-witting the opposition that we face in life.Rev.22:13

The Clubs That We Get Hit With

A man setting in a doctor's office waiting to see him was suddenly startled to see another man rushed in without an appointment to see HIS private doctor who looked badly beaten and bloody though maybe not serious enough to have been sent to the local E.R. yet still injured accompanied by what looked like family members who sat next him.

Curious, not trying to be nosey the young man waiting before the wounded man arrived, concerned but tactful ask the family member(s): "Excuse me, but I know maybe I shouldn't ask this but, "What happen to him?"

The family member nearest him began to tell him: "Well he had given his best friend a new golf club about a month ago but they had an argument today while playing a round of golf and he took that SAME CLUB and beat him over the head with it!

That man came out of the doctor's office about a half an hour later bandaged, bruised, damaged and sore but otherwise ok but wiser. It bought to light a quote my father used to say to me son: "A still tongue makes a wise head. Never give a man a stick to hit you over the head with son. Let him find his own!"

This analogy is almost a no brainer or you'll have NONE IN YOUR HEAD TO THINK WITH! ..(lol).. Often the clubs that we get our worst beat downs with, are the ones gave to others in the forms of TRUST by confiding in them our personal pains, struggles, and drama which meant they knew both our strengths and our weaknesses.

AND WITH OUR WEAKNESSES they in turn use them to OPPRESS US WITH! They were given POWER OVER US BY THE INFORMATION WE GAVE THEM.

All too often "The Clubs That We Get Hit With" are the ones we give as gifts of trust and love and then they are turned into weaponry in anger by those we them share with. Being careless with our love with those who are thought to be our friends sometimes they turn on us and HURT US WITH THAT POWER!!

That is why prayer to God only is so important. It's the club of respect and love from someone we can admire and who will never get so angry with us even when we error, He will still lovingly embarrass us and our gift of sharing. If there's only one lesson to gain from this epiphany get it quickly! People can and will hurt you but often it's because we gave them:" The Clubs That We Get Hit With".Ps.118:1-17.

The Art of Shadow Boxing

Boxers have for years trained for fights that they are not even scheduled to fight or that are so far off in their distant futures simply by doing a series of regime(s). Tactics handed down for generations. They do weight training, running, jogging, watch their diet(s), what they drink, even their sex lives come into play all because. They want to be ready when or if a fight comes: SOONER THAN EXPECTED!!!But the most essential drill that they practice is: "The Art of Shadow Boxing."

The art form that allows them to go beyond how they've trained before to imagine they are in the fight and fighting an opponent they are NOT YET FACING.! The reason for this is to insure their state of readiness at any time PREPARING FOR THE UNXPECTED.

Some have gotten so good at it that they can hardly if ever be surprised at any time by: an angry person, gang or gang-member, bouncer, or rival ever hitting them without the appropriate counter to defend themselves.

Being ready and well abled to defend one's self in the times we live in are almost imperative nowadays but there's another form of shadow boxing that absolutely demands that same level of dedication and commitment as well.

It is called: YOUR PRAYER LIFE. Jesus practice it at the Mount of Temptation being tempted by the Devil but was ready for him when he appeared because prayer BEFORE problems come, equips us with spiritual reflexes that become second nature to us to avoid knock-outs, being hit below the belt, sucker bunches, rabbit bunches, and even if they slip in they won't take us out.

Pre-training we are always ready because we are not perfect. "The Art of Shadow Boxing having learned from the Master Himself taught us through prayer."

Prayer IS shadow boxing! And practice makes perfect .The perfect resolve too, for those who practice it, for those who battle because of their trainer's skill-set which always insures THEY WIN...!!! Mt.26:37-41, Eph.6:14-18, Lk. 18:1-8.

Why....The Stress-Test?

A young man goes to his doctor for an annual physical, getting the usual things done: Ears nose, throat, lungs, x-rays. Thinking now it was ok to go home, his doctor then said to him: Bobby Joe, got one more thing I need to give you (A STRESS TEST)! To which Bobby objected because he ran, lifted weights, did aerobics all of which he felt most assuredly insured his good health but the doctor insisted upon a stress test.

A stress test? "Why....The Stress-Test" Doc? Bobby asked. The doctor said; "I'll tell you when I'm done!" So he hooked him up, then placed him on the treadmill to elevate his heart-rate. That's when the doctor raised the speed to an alarming rate 'til Bobby shouted: Stop doc.! Stop! You're about to kill me!!! But It was Ignored by the doctor.

Then when the doctor was satisfied that he was ok, he lowered the speed, then stopped it altogether. Breathing hard and now very angry, Bobby Joe fussed and became enraged. Once he was calm, his doctor walked unto the dressing room where he proceeded to get dressed and then explained to him why. "Why... The Stress-Test"? "Bobby he said,: I did this because of the demands and at the request of your employer. He has plans to place you in an executive capacity and He, unbeknownst to you, needed to know could handle

17

what lies ahead of you in the future so that's why. "Why... The Stress-Test!!! If you could not endure it, then you are not ready for promotion. >>It's that simple. <<!

God, in order to promote us, must test us though He already knows the outcome!!!!! The test is not for His approval. It's for our strength to handle what is in store for us. It's the last test prior to promotion. Once He sees we are ready through the hardest part of success BEFORE SUCCESS it is then are we told it's intent, then there is only joy in the promotion.

God wants us to be happy but He must test us through the strain and rigors of life with what makes us want to quit and give up. So when life gets extremely difficult, day-break and promotion are next. So like Bobby asked Him. Ask Him why the stress test(s)? When it's all over, only then you'll appreciate the exercise. That's why. Why... The Stress-Test"!!!!!   Jn.16:19-28,   Js.1:2-9, Jer.29:11&12, 2Tim.2:1-5, Rom.5:1-5, Ps.30:5!

God Won't Put You on Speaker Phone

I think people sometimes think that other people are not as smart as they think they are OR they underestimate their own LACK OF PERCEPTION about them that others readily pick up on.

Case in point. A guy was who talking to a supposed friend, ON A CELL PHONE secretly then put him on speaker phone during what was THOUGHT TO BE A PRIVATE CONVERSATION THEY WERE HAVING only to try to embarrass him to the people in the area where he was to allow them to have the opportunity to be able to LISTEN TO THE WHOLE THING.

So while he THOUGHT he was leading his so called friend down the path to privately humiliate him, he didn't realize that the SOUND the speaker phone made when it's (turned on) is totally different than when NOT!! Which clued him that: OTHERS ARE BEING (possibly) ALLOWED TO ... listen in. The friend never knew til he told him later that he had a speaker phone too and knew the game or trick that was being played on him.

Their relationship changed instantly from that day forward because privacy is: As PRECIOUS as gold and when violated, the value of trust is GONE FOREVER!

The object in this case scenario was an issue of SUPERIOR one friend, based on how ONE over estimated HIMSELF while underestimating THE WISDOM OF THE OTHER but "God Won't Put You On Speaker Phone or loud talk you at others expense.

He only wants to bless us...not curse us with the scrutiny of other listening ears. TO PROVE A POINT THAT HE IS BETTER THAN US!!!!

What we say to Him is PRIVATE NO MATTER WHAT WE HAVE DONE, IT IS KEPT CONFIDENTIAL...ALL because "God Won't Put You on Speaker Phone" Ps.32:1-6.

Under the Black-Light

I grew up in the 70's. Music was the going things and parties too. Whenever you'd get invited to a party back in those day, expect to see afros, bell-bottom pants, lamps, paisley colors and be entertained often: "Under the Black Light".

They were ultra-violet lights like those used in a film developing room in that day and time and today used to do forensic investigations at crime scenes. They only light up anything that would otherwise go un-noticed under normal lighting conditions.

What makes the black light so special is that it set the mood for the next thing(s) about to happen. Usually people invited would sit and socialize in the dark. See when someone entered the room, IT'S PITCH BLACK and the only way those coming in got noticed was by what stood out on them IN THE DARK. "Under the Black Light!".

Adjacent to that room was a well-lit room where the food and music was waiting once all who were invited had arrived. If you had not shaved, or wore certain kinds of jewelry, had on something that had glitter on it, light colored clothing, lip-gloss or anything with lint on it, dust or dirt even make-up, it would show up: "Under the Black Light".

Black lights showed all the excess or imperfections at the party that stand out on all who take the invitations to come to the party (YET ON ONE THERE FEELS EMBARRASSED) because something shows up in the dark in God's presence and technically WE ARE ALL UNDER GOD'S BLACK LIGHT. See ultraviolet light is a part of all light period!

God sees us day or night and our sins, though hidden show up in his presence and the good part is His mercy invited us to not feel guilty about our imperfections at the party. That is what going to God in prayer is like daily. You'll understand it better by reading this scripture when you get time: "Under the Black Light." Of devotion. Heb.4:12-16, 1Jn.1:5-9.

I Know It Was The Blood

A school in an urban community was attacked by a lunatic seeking revenge for a fight he had gotten into years before so he took an automatic assault weapon to kill as many people as he could before the police arrived committing suicide. Leaving families devastated and because the paramedics told them when they came there NO ONE SURVIVED THE INCIDENT. But one lone child came out in front as a news caster broadcasted the sad news.

Shocked, they ran to get him finding that he was unharmed. While they reported his words live to everyone watching the show. When asked by them how he survived it he said: "When I saw all my classmates falling from gun-fire, and before the bullets got to me , I fell too and when the gunman turned as he heard the police arriving, I covered my body with the blood of those around me who I knew were dead and when he returned to where I was, and began to shoot everybody again to make sure that they were dead. If he saw they were breathing so (I HELD MY BREATH) and breathed through my mouth slowing with my eyes closed which made him think I was already dead, and as he past, me, he began to shoot those remaining 'til he got to the end then he turned the gun on himself before the police got in the door. !!!!"I Know It Was The Blood"!!!! that saved me. See somebody else's blood SAVED

MY LIFE. I JUST USED IT AND SURRENDER AND EVIL PASSED ME BY.

That's what Jesus did for us. He took the bullet that was meant to take me out as I fell in His blood ALIVE BEFORE Death came to claim my life . !!!!" I Know It Was The Blood"!!!!! Shed just for me that kept me alive. As I died a FAKE death by using it.

Surrendered to the shed blood gave me a new chance to live again. That's what salvation is like through Christ's blood. Just fall down in prayer, play dead to the world then cover yourself with His blood meant to save anyone who uses it.

Ask any person who believes. They will tell you what saved them. They will like the child TESTIFY." I Know It Was The Blood"! That is what they know about the Cross at Calvary. Jn.3:5-18,Exod.12:5-11,G.I.G.A.T.T.

The Danger of A Misdiagnosis

Ever known anyone whose gone to the doctor and given a pill, ointment, shot, treatment and they end up having an erratic behavioral reaction to them all because the symptoms said one thing when the treatment demanded something else!

People have died all because they were given the wrong remedy to a problem that seem to require one thing, but given something totally different! The reason that is, is because so many problems have similar symptoms and so many test have to be run just to make sure a person survives and recovers from what is troubling them.

Ever been given bad advice? Judged incorrectly? Insulted all because someone thought that was the remedy to FIX YOU? All with the soul deliberate intent that THEY know more about you than God does, your family, friends, associates or anyone does?

They labeled you based on what they... SAW .... Heard...and or Perceived about you. BUT THEY NEVER KNEW YOU PERSONALLY. Intimately, relevantly. They only make matters worse on you NOT BETTER!!

What you then suffer from is the supposed CURE THEIR JUDGMENTS OF YOU have prescribed!!! Though you may not know what is wrong with you, there is no doubt you know what is RIGHT. That being, a need to be understood. There is a CURE FOR IT...IT IS CALLED PRAYER.

There was a woman in the Bible who spent all she had on a doctor's treatment and yet she suffered an enormously LONG TIME!!!! 'Til she ran into Jesus and only touched the hem of His garment...(WHERE NO SENSITIVITY IS)... Yet He felt her. For she said WITHIN HERSELF "if I but touch His garment, I will be made whole...Mt.9:20&21.

Time is fast teaching me not to trust people for the cures to what ails me. That way, there won't be >>>>The Danger of A Misdiagnosis<<<< but: There Is A Balm Gilead. Jer.8:22 Prayer .....AND IT WILL NEVER GIVE A MISDIAGNOSIS ....A CURE that will give you PEACE....in the process.

The Psychology of Spite

I was very...very fortunate in my life to have a great father... who taught me lots of life lessons and also a very great mentor who was both a minister and a psychology major in college. I learned both knowledge of God, also how and why the human mind functions like it does.

Out of all the lessons I learned from him, my mentor, I learned how to understand what the human mind is sometimes secretly up to, by it's behavioral pattern(s)

I was having a hard time given to me by people that I had never done anything to personally, and I couldn't understand why and he explained it to me this way. In layman's terms: "The Psychology Of Spite."

First, spite is a behavior rooted in some form of insecurity or a low self-esteem. Hence it is compensating for itself by the torture and or humiliation of someone usually undeserving of the penalization. They then become the victim of that person's insecurity, and usually they try to make them paid a penalty just because they think they are empowered to do so and it is rooted in envy .

In short, it is a bullying tactic coming from an inferiority complex which is usually rooted in their childhood from never being or not feeling adequate or are unloved and if that person (their target) has

Anything they themselves lack or covets,or whatever that person needs from them, they make it their business to do to them totally the opposite in their treatment of them. So every chance they get they try to make them pay for their OWN personal problems.

Once you understand their motive then you operate in the "REVERSE PSYCHOLOGY" by ignoring their efforts to annoy you. He said to me: Love your enemies and it will totally confuse them and cause them to examine themselves more than they make problems for you.

Pray for those who spitefully misuse you. That will cause them to re-assess themselves and leave the rest to God. Fighting your battles is HIS JOB. Not your's and ask the Lord to forgive (THEM OF THEMSELVES) as you do so you both win!. That is the perfect strategy for victory...with "The Psychology of Spite"....Rom.12:9-21..Mt.5:43-48, Lk.6:27-36.

<u>Friends Have Friends</u>

A bought lesson is the best lesson. It's what you pay but it's what pay WITH ....is where the cost comes in. Let me explain it like this: Two people were suffering from same addiction went to drug counseling where they were in groups with a variety of people suffering from the same problem all trying to overcome it. They had to stand, say their names and admit they were an....????...(question mark) on purpose!!!

After they confessed their issues, aired out their dirty laundry, one to another, suggested and offered help one to another, feeling relieved their therapist ended the session with this remarks: Be careful when you leave here to whom you share this information. My reason is so simple. "Friends Have Friends" THAT ARE NOT YOUR FRIENDS! And when or if you shared something confidential, those who are THEIR FRIENDS will mercilessly condemn you just for being honest, and by not factoring in the domino effect then it make things insurmountable. Then EVERYBODY will know your business. The pain you then will endure if you are not strong will either make you stronger or wound or break your spirit so to the point you will trust no one.

But that is GOOD In a way especially if you have faith in God.

Why because your level of trust in Him gets higher and makes man of none affect. That is how I as a counselor, have survived. I can trust God in prayer. He is a friend that understands what man CAN NOT...

It's THAT... (Trust Factor) you have to factor in that most people don't. God is not like us. He keeps it to Himself. He wants you to tell others especially it's confidential! That way everyone will seek Him.

That is the kind of friend we all need when "Friends Have Friends" Be his fiend and let Him BE YOURS. The good dynamic of when: "Friends Have Friends".

Hence, the question mark. What's your addition? Now: Who's YOUR FRIEND? Ps.55:1-22, Ps.118:1-9, Prov.18:24, Prov.17:17, Prov. 27:6.

<u>Stuck In a Holding Pattern</u>

Two things commonly happen to both Cargo and Transport aircraft during their routine flights from arrival to final destinations. They are more often than we count or even take notice of, required by the inbound plane terminals instructed to remain UP IN THE AIR. Don't forget that part. Told by those who control traffic to circle the airport due to: weather conditions, accidents, congestion, terroristic threats, hoaxes, power outages, under staffing, computer malfunctions, medical emergencies etc. Just to name a few.

So decisions have to be made for flights due to arrive or depart the terminals. With those factors being considered and that is never done before factoring in: HOW MUCH FUEL THEY HAVE REMAINING.

I love to parallel life in the same ways because after we have come on a long journey...THROUGH IT, we can't always arrive when we want to or even disembark SOMETIMES we get: "Stuck In a Holding Pattern" by the inbound tower for reasons only the PILOTS AND CREW KNOW ABOUT while we're left UP IN THE AIR. Wondering why he delay.

In life I have been left hanging sometimes not always knowing why I can't get where I feel I need to be, though I've paid my FAIR (what was due of me) Ooops! Fare Misspelled on purpose: My FARE, yet I am being deliberately prevented from landing on time by MY TIMETABLE but the good thing about being stuck ALL UP IN THE AIR IS, they always land you (even at another airport) BEFORE they let you crash!!

God, when we pray about the next steps in life by His oversight, already knows where He's going to place us before we crash, by boarded His Aircraft.

It's His duty to unsure our safety and arrival. That's what TRUST IS.! Believing in the CARRIER. Knowing we will surely not be left, hanging or up in the air about our fate in the end. So when in doubt remember this scripture: Jer.29:11-14...and pray this one:Ps.61:1-8 whenever you are: "Stuck In a Holding Pattern".

The House Always Wins

Scenario: The largest jackpot in casino history was won by a one spin of a slot-machine in Vegas. 20 MILLION dollars was awarded to a homeless man who pan-handled there in the city for years where he had gotten his monies where he lived off of from people passing by on the strip.

Now wealthy beyond his wildest dreams bought a house, made some good investments and lived comfortably 'til his death.

The casino where he won later was interviewed after his win and prior to his death after his win the owner of the casino spoke freely about the record breaking news/making event. He was asked: Did your losing so much all at once affect your business where you felt taken back a large loss so suddenly? Did it cause you to lose customers? Did you lose assets? He replied laughing: "Of course not. Here's why".

The money he won was only SOME OF A MONEY thousands and ten's of thousands of people here have wagered their life's earnings for years and years before he had played and LOST IT ALL WHERE HE WON, but the real winner here is THE CASINO ITSELF because he won a very small percentage. We figure over the years we've made at least 20 times that much because the odds are always in the owner's favor. Simply put: He won a small portion of what others losers lost. We got the rest. See "The House Always Wins"! If it didn't we couldn't stay in business and our business is to always COME OUT AHEAD!

When Jesus died on the Cross, in some ways, there is a similarity to this because God the father invested in His Son's death as a win because He died and won us for His Father who runs, owns and manages things.

Though Satan hits the jackpot occasionally, he will never breaks the house, rules, overtakes or runs the HOUSE because the odds are FROM ETERNITY...are ALWAYS IN GOD 'S FAVOR.

Let not your heart be trouble by those who are playing the game for gain with God's money. IT WILL BE SHORT-LIVED, because: "The House Always Wins." No matter how the game is played or who plays it or what's at stake. They might get by but they will never get away. He built it to be indestructible.BECAUSE WE GAMBLES ON HIM IN GOOD FAITH.
So when we go to Him in prayer, It's HIS HOUSE...WE NEVER LOSE... WHEN HE WINS, Knowing WHEN WE PRAY that either win or lose at God's table with the right motive, "The House Always Win." Mt.21:12&13, Mt.16:12-18, Ps.127:1-5.....!

What Do You Do...When The Joke's On You?

In life, I have notice that there is a distinct difference between TELLING A JOKE, AND Lastly being the (THE BUTT OF A JOKE). There to me is nothing more malicious or mean-spiritedly done than having a joke played on you to mock you...and it all be done completely and obviously to your not being aware of it.

But what about when you KNOW it's being {played on you} yet those who do it are CLUELESS that you are ...... So ooh.. CLUED IN... AND ... YET THEY HAVE NO IDEA YOU KNOW!

In such a case as that, "What Do You... When The Joke's On You? Sometimes the wisdom of it all is to: "LET 'EM PULL IT OFF" repetitively and while everyone is snickering behind your back about embarrassing you ...YOU SUFFER THROUGH IT....!

Now some would say: Don't get mad, Get Even. Play a joke right back ON THEM, but if your life is filled with Prayer, you can see it before it comes and it be no shock to you at all.

There is a Divine Method to the MADNESS OF MADNESS IN THIS CASE, it's to simply (Recognize the motive). That motive deductively reasoned out leaves only ONE CONCLUSION. That the kind of joke being played on you was for one reason only SPITE. Spite translated only means: JUST BECAUSE I CAN.

Now spite is done solely for the purpose of celebration of empowerment. Bullies do it, battered wives experience it, corporate execs and Wall Street entrepreneurs use this tactic to: they think psychologically gain advantage and sometimes it's meant solely to make sport of someone thought to be of lesser importance but after it is done so frequently, it only EXPOSES THE JOKESTER …. TO THE PERSON ON WHO THE JOKE IS BEING PLAYED.!!!!

There is a story told of a little boy with a sign stuck on his back which read: KICK ME! and the people who read it, did it for a while but afterward they became more conscience of how wrong it was, accept for this ONE guy!Who continued it relentlessly while the rest of the school's children watched stunned and ashamed. But each time the boy who was being kicked simply fell to his knees and wept briefly then would get up and continue on his way until a by-stander shouted to him:" Why aren't you defending yourself?! He tearfully replied: I AM defending myself.

While those who taunted him, taunted on as they listened to him. How? The spectator cried! You are still allowing this to continue. He smiled through his tears and said (BY PRAYING FOR THOSE WHO SPITEFULLY MISUSE ME).

And no sooner than he said it, the mockery of him stopped. Because those who had made him the butt of their private celebration were looked upon in shame!

So no matter how we are done in life and before you attempt to fight back or play a joke back on those who persecute you, remember what Jesus both said and DID HIMSELF, HE PRAYED FOR THEM...THE JOKE WAS FINALLY PLAYED ON THEM. By THE RESURRECTION...VICTORY!!

Now that's the answer to the question of: "What Do You When The Joke's On You"!!!!! Ps.69:1-13, Mt.5:43-45, Lk.6:27-36.

<u>Something for Nothing</u>

Me and a friend were at a fast-food restaurant having a conversation and a meal when I noticed (what was thought to be a panhandler approaching our table) so before he arrived there, I warned my friend of his approach. Upon arriving at our table he showed me a dollar then asked for something to eat. So I asked him: "What do you want to eat? I'll buy you something to eat.!! "He replied: "A hamburger, fries and a drink." I then replied: "Ok, give me your dollar to put with it and I'll buy it for you."!!! He became somewhat hostile and refused my offer COMPLETELY

See, what he wanted was for me to meet his needs, do all the work, yet make no sacrifices himself, but was not willing to contribute to the process! Later he fooled someone on the outside and kept coming back hassling prospective customers the same way. Then looked at me and shouted: "I don' t want anything you've got" My reply was: And I don't want anything you've got either"!!! He wanted "Something for Nothing".

My father taught me this phrase:" Give a man a fish, you feed him for a day. Teach a man to fish and you feed him for life." It's amazes me how we sometimes expect things from others as if we are entitled to them. Almost as if we are in some ways are supposed to possess things that we full well know what we want belongs to them.

We want dollars we never earned, food we never cooked. Cars and houses we never paid cars or house notes for. Even clothes because they fit us and worse, we have no intention of ever putting in the work those we expect these things from have. Nor do we even consider it our duty to personally make things happen for ourselves Never realizing the pattern of getting "Something for Nothing" cripples us and makes us dependent upon assistance that then becomes an addition and because we have received it for such long time without working for it, then becomes psychologically blind to the reality of labor and live in denial then we blame those who don't give us what we want...by not making THINGS HAPPEN FOR OURSELVES. So that is expected. "Something FOR SOMETHING...

Beg God. Then be prepared to labor for it. Prayer gives us answers but also requires even demands that we work to make our dreams a reality. "Something for Nothing." The grace aspect but we work BECAUSE WE ARE SAVED BY GRACE Thus making our something special.Now that's really SOMETHING. Check these out They are really something. Acts 3:1-12...2 Thess.3:1-13...Jn.9:1-14.... G.I.G.A.T.T.

Kaleidoscope

A man trying to cheer up his son after he had lost a baseball championship game, a (tiny league) game bought him a: "Kaleidoscope". He had never seen one before and needed an explanation of it, how it worked and what to do with it.

So his father explained it to him and said: "It's a tube made with mirrors, colored glass fragments, that when shaken and held a certain way, it makes beautiful pictures. Then said to his son, try it and see for yourself.

So he shook it and held it down toward the ground and said to his father: "It doesn't work daddy. Why did you get me this?" His father smiled and said. "Son, you must point it to the sky" So he did and to his surprise, he saw the most beautiful collection of colors he had ever seen. Then he said I feel much better daddy. Thank you for the wonderful present dad but how did you know it would make me feel better? He said, Easy.!!

It's like life son, we lose sometimes and we look at the fragments like our failures. Head down, through a small opening and no light in sight. But when we shake 'em up, TILT THEM TO THE SKY AND AIM THEM AT (the Sun a.k.a. the Son), LET THE LIGHT SHINE ON THEM they somehow make sense and form a beautiful picture of all things working together for good.

Simply because we are looking in right directions where failures, fragments and futures, all make perfect sense in the light >OF THE SON.< When it's aimed in the upward direction of the altar! Rom.8:28, Jer.29:11-15....G.I.G.A.T.T.

I'm In Here Too

A man, rushing to get his wife to a very important engagement where time was a priority and they were running late, was driving like there was no tomorrow and was swerving, even speeding, riding, tailgating cars ahead of him to get her there on time for her appointment. Then she said: "Slow down! You ARE GOING TO ME KILLED" To which he replied: "Baby Chill" I got this. I know exactly what I'm doing and besides you forget two very important things. She said: "And what's that??? He then responded very calmly: 1. "I'm driving." and 2. "I'm In Here Too and I am just as (if not more) important than you and I'm not going to do anything to hurt me. That's what keep us safe!"

How often WE FORGET when we are going through something while trying to get where we need to be in life somtimes causes us to panic about how things look to us on our journey through life.

When we pray about things that distress us we sometimes think God doesn't really care about the dangers that frighten us because when we pray (WE GIVE HIM THE POWER TO GET US THERE ON TIME SAFELY). Though we are aware of it we are being selfish not factoring in His Skills as the driving force behind our badly needed resolve of the problems we face.

So take it from me and my own personal experience when I pray. He reminds me not to panic and says calmly to my soul. "I'm Driving So Chill"!! "I'm In Here Too"! and He's not going to harm himself. We did that to Him already AT THE CROSS and say Peace Be Still. "I'm In Here Too"

Mt.8:23-27,….Dan.6:18-22,Ps.46:1-11,Dan.3:12-25 25,Jer.29:11&12,Cor.10:13.

A Copy ...From The Master-Copy

I have lots of music at home. Of every genre, type, and some even on vinyl albums old and new. But due to the latest technology, usually duplicate almost all of it because experience as taught me that after loaning out some, losing some, and sadly having some borrowed and never returned or even some stolen so having extra copies keeps me with the bulk of my music still intact.

So now when people ask me for some of it for whatever purpose or reason without thinking about it twice, I just make them: "A Copy...From the Master-Copy(s)"! that way, everybody ends up SATISFIED.

Now they don't get the originals just a copy of it. See the perks from keeping the Master Copy for myself is: It's PERFECT...WITHOUT A STRATCH....! I can make as many duplicates from the Master as necessary for an unlimited amount of people for many varied reasons to do with them whatever they want and if they lose, break, or damage them, I can make them another. So having the Master is everything to reproduction because it's flawless, enduring, and lastly renewing for others. That's what MASTERS DO!!!They Replicate!

Let me stretch your imagination for a second. Did you ever think of yourself through DNA as being a carbon copy from a perfect source? Thus being "A

Copy...From The Master-Copy? God the Father and His Son being the Master Copy and made you and I replicas of Himself in His Image and after His Likeness. So that being the truth, what happens to us when we get lost, broken, borrowed, misplace or just flat-out stolen or scratched up or not returned to the one who owns us.

You can be REPRODUCED! We called it: Restoration ...Reduplication to who or what we once were. The old one gets trashed and a new one gets recreated. All we have to do is: Go back to the SOURCE OF YOUR ORIGIN, YOUR MASTER and ask Him for another RE-MAKE.

In other words, get: "A Copy... From The Master-Copy. God can even after you've been lost, scratched, or misplaced or just not working properly remake us.

Just ask for what we call in layman's terms: ANOTHER CHANCE, and He will give you a do-over, a remake, a clone, a copy. The old you made BRAND NEW. All because you PRAYED realizing the old copy doesn't work anymore and the best you can be reborn as: "a Copy...From The Master's Master-Copy"! Phil.2:5-11, Gen.1:25-31, Rom.12:1&2, 1 Jn.1:3-10.

The Reading of The Will

A large family had gathered themselves together for "The Reading Of The Will" OF A NOW DECEASED yet beloved family member who had recently past away.

One by one their names came up and what was then bequeathed them as heirs, all seemingly expectant of his or her apparent wealth and after about the twentieth one was named, there was a hush that came over the rest of them because this one was thought to inherit the remaining bulk of the estate but when their name was called, the attorney's tone became somewhat vindictive and harsh as he called their name.

He said: "And to you, after carefully consideration of all you have done to in this position, I leave you NOTHING. The reason being, you were dishonest, deceitful, expectant, and merciless in your quest to endear yourself to me all because you thought you could reap the benefits when you never truly loved or cared for me. You only wanted what you thought being with me would net you...You lied, hurt people, stole and manipulated yourself into position(s) to hopefully benefit your own future which left the others shocked because they thought it went un-noticed but everyone knew it.

See wills are sometimes more than inheritances .They are ADHERENCES ....Wills are OUR....(DO RIGHTS)!!!AND are.........NOT our DUE-LY Expected REWARDS...because there is no will left for us, when it's God's will for us to do right thing >>>BY OTHERS<<<.When we fail to do what is right to stay in God's...WILL...for our lives...and we get NO REWARD INTO ETERNITY because we fail to value that it's part of His will that we treat each other honestly!

The will here has a double meaning because it's gaged in how we treat each other. Some of us will be sadly disappointed when Jesus calls our names because we have knowingly hurt, injured neglected or destroyed others for the sake of ill gotten gain.

Our prayer life brings us into self-examination and causes us to question our motives by simply asking God to search us. That is in: "The Reading of The Will" His Perfect Will. >>>THE BIBLE<<<to only discover where we truly stand.

Pray and study ....to get the benefits of BOTH...Rom.12:1&2,1Thes.5:1-18,Mic.6:1-9,Mt.25:31-46 Ps.139:22-24.

Trippin'

The term: "Trippin" is a 70's expression given to people who were thought to be or known to be, on some form of drugs like: LSD, ANGELDUST, MARIJUANA, SPEED, or some hallucinogenic that causes the user(s) to see things that are simply NOT THERE! But suppose someone said or implied that about you, when you were clinically sane all because you saw some things that they were unable to see or conceive as reality? Suppose even further that you had what some would call: Second sight, or even a supernatural gift or ability that causes you to see, YEARS INTO THE FUTURE.

And though you tried to share that with people, but all because it hasn't happened yet, because (THEY ARE IN THE MOMENT), and even when they to whom you share it all with are in the moment, when they themselves are sometimes intricately involved in what you SEE, it would make you second guess yourself. Even not trusting of people nor yourself especially when what you see almost always comes true.

Well if that happens to you as I just described, people would say that you are just "Trippin"! They would privately mock you feel, sorry for you or pity you and say you have a metal disorder and yet have no idea that you KNOW IT also ALL IN ADVANCE. They just don't know it and you can't never let on to them that you know, even though from time to time you try to explain it to them, they just get don't it and you also know that too.

But they are 100% right.... You ARE "Trippin". If your relationship with God through prayer is strong, then you are on a spiritual journey beyond time and space. You through prayer and meditation to God are just being given a prepared visit in your NOW..., TO THE ... THEN.

This happens to me from time to time. At first it frustrated me then I realized through prayer why. Why am I just "Trippin"? Then finally He told me this way. Don. this is done so that nothing will ever take you by surprise. I HAVE INSULATED YOU...WITH A BUILT IN SHOCK ABSORBER that nothing will surprise you by anyone.

I did that to Joseph so he could handle the hardships that were going to come his way. It's not new. IT'S JUST FAVOR! And you only get hurt when you don't pay attention and like Joseph, your future is bright. Tell everyone that they too can start... "Trippin" this way TOO!

Just seek my presence THROUGH PRAYER.. And just like Joseph and many others ...IT CAN HAPPEN TO THEM too. IT'S CALLED: PROPHESY a.k.a. "Trippin" and when the journey finally ends, you'll be glad you were "Trippin", and your ability to handle things meant to hurt you, will leave those who try to ..You guessed it: "Trippin"! Gen.37:1-10,Gen.45:1-7,Is.43:1-13.

Who Wins

I vividly remember a heavy weight fight where the two fighters fighting each other were independently asked in separate interviews !!!!!"
Who Wins"? When they fight each other. They (both men of faith and prayer) claimed that God told them by answering them the same thing, their response to the interviewer:" I believe I will" But in truth ,there can only be one winner right? What then would determine the final outcome? Simple: THE WILL OF GOD FOR BOTH OF THEM.!!!!

See , faith was not the determining factor here. Neither their skill or work ethic. Nor their strength nor power or experience. It's what God Himself had to say about it that honors His Will …. That is what determines how things turn out period.!!!!

People have tendencies to pray selfishly rather than: What IS the will of God. The love of what God wants more than ours shows the desire for obedience, not dominance. With the power of God being supreme as the determiner of the one's who're fighting. It is the good fight of faith which has losses riddled all through it. So there will be no sore losers even when we prayed and believe that we would win. That way, what has determined: "Who Wins"? has (NO LOSERS BECAUSE VICTORY IS ALWAYS GOD'S)

So whether you win or lose a fight or not you still WIN!!!If the ingredients in prayer included what God wants. We who pray always win. That's what God really wants in our lives. His Will.

The who wins? God does when the victory in us is Him !!!.1 Jn.5:4-15 ..Jn. 15:1-15..Luke 22:39-42..Rom.8:14-27....Mt.6:9&10....G.I.G.A.T.T.

LONG

Like most people, I have a lot of questions about things I just don't understand, but differently from most people...I DON'T ASK PEOPLE FOR ANSWERS OFTEN. I ask God HIMSELF.

While dealing with a problem the relentlessly crippled my life (that wasn't even mine in no sense of the word yet was relentlessly disruptive) I asked Him why He had left it to linger in my life so LONG. When He could have fixed it easily and quickly. Why it left those nearest to me blinded to it's affects. Why was He taking so LONG to deal with it while He also constrained me from taking matters into my own hands to resolve it years ago and this He is what He spoke back to my mind concerning the problem.

I need to build a resume on you that will pay dividends but I am also building a resume on those who are deliberately offending you. See they think they are getting away when they are merely GETTING BY while building up a LONG resume just like yours. Unlike yours however, because yours is being built by me. While the enemy is using them though they belong to me and before they leave this Earth they will pay a LONG time for the evil they have sown in your life deliberately.

Hence the word: LONG-SUFFERING is built on my Love NOT YOURS! Yours lack the power of the Spirit. Mine IS THE SPIRIT. By this all men will know you are mine if you have LOVE for one another. I need an example of:
"ME IN YOU" THAT BY YOUR STANDARDS IS TAKING TOO LONG. By mine it's nothing.

I see the end but you see the struggle. What you don't see is that others see it too, and wonder if you are blind to it...but THEY ARE RIGHT! because you don't react to it.

Love is blind. Look at what they did to Me and I didn't do anything to them either. Must Jesus bare the Cross alone and all the world go free? For there's a Cross for EVERYONE and there's a Cross for THEE!!! See judgment against wickedness is not executed swiftly because I AM LONG-SUFFERING ...BUT EXACT because I allow space to repent because those who making it hard for you: "KNOW that they are making it hard for you"

What they don't know is IT IS NOT WITHOUT PENALTY.

Patience is dictated by: The Wisdom of Time. Time By Space...Space By Knowledge and knowledge, by: The Wisdom Of Consequence ...and everyone's penalty(s)will hinge on the warning of conscience they willfully receive and ignore.

Stay in prayer for them knowing my judgement is sure and without remedy and also the resume rewards us all accordingly...LONG after they thought to be forgotten.

Gal.6:5-12...1Cor.13:4-10...Ps.37:1-11...35-40..PET.3:8-15...G.I.G.A.T.T.

Salvation

The Be All To End All! The statement more often than not used to describe the personal conceit of those who are also, (more often than not) the believing that they are deciding factor(s) on whether they think someone should be something, get something, do something or not...IF THEY HAVE ANYTHING TO SAY ABOUT IT! They, because of power or influences believe they are the determining forces whether someone fails or succeeds. But far worse are those who fail their value of themselves, not realizing they have the power to redeem themselves from the prison(s) they are placed in by those who are sure that their "Salvation" their rescuer, their redeemer, or savior depends on them.

How blind we sometimes become by the positions of power we are given as if we have the final say over whether someone lives or dies or goes or stays when we neither created them or own them.

The question then becomes: Who do we trust to be our source of survival in any crisis that we are confronted with. "Salvation" is a term use to deliver us from whatever it is we face that is meant to hinder us. Stop relying on a person or system or authority to determine your fate when REAL "Salvation" is a FAITH BASED ingredient that gives us hope WITHOUT HUMAN INTERVENTION!...

I have seen people use their money, influence, or authority to hurt people who have done nothing to deserve it. Using a God given gift bestowed on them now feeling their mercy only is what is needed to help or hinder people when they themselves were given it by grace not entitlement.

We can pray as God's children and receive anything we ask if it's in the will of God and man can do nothing about it. Who are you relying on as YOUR "Salvation"?

Well if you are still on lock-down from your future success, then the only one to blame is YOU! Man can't stop you because Jesus IS your "Salvation" but you must believe He can and will save you from any bondage and bind those who try to bind you not realizing He is their "Salvation" Too! So if you feel bound just PRAY TO HIM and discover what most of us already know... True "Salvation" IS IN THE HANDS OF GOD!!!! Dan.6:8-22.... Heb.11:6, Dan.3:22-30, Ps.35:1-28, Ps.27:1-15, Acts.4:1-12, Ps.40:1-6.

The One's I Get Wrong

Was playing an online trivia game. Been playing it for a short while now. It is multiple choice so it's hit or miss depending on one's level of knowledge, skill or instinct about what could be the right answer. Sometimes I'm dead on but more often than not, I'm Wrong.!!! Embarrassingly so. I have learned to except my lack of knowledge but the game inspires me so for one basic reason: "The Ones I Get Wrong" are the constant reminders I don't know everything about things I feel well versed in.

The test of the game exposes me to myself even if no one else knows my answer(s). I am then left to brood or to take it all in stride, taking note of what the right answer(s) ARE. What that does not only informs me, it makes me SMARTER ABOUT MY ERRORS!!!

Life is a game of a similar sort. It tests us to see if we can find the ways of knowledge about it. That requires I study more recognize, change and increase and get better because I remember my failures. "The Ones I Get Wrong". So as to not do them again. A famous quote I heard once said: "Those who have not learned from the past, are destined to repeat it"

Life can be like a trivia game though it should never be taken trivially. Those sins I thought were the right things to do I thought were right turned out were WRONG.!! Prayer with God's answers to the questions helps me to check the right boxes and leaves the inquiry for more trivia with God and one who has all the right answers. Sometimes after the choices have already been made.

Pray for guidance because the choices can be costly but once you have errored. He still gives you the right answer. He's got all of them and more and learn from our mistakes, the fewer we will make as we continue to play or pray. Correcting some things. Like "The One's I Get Wrong". It's called repentance. Lk.18:10-14 Ps.119: 65-72, Lk.15:17-24, Prov.3:5-1.

Stuck In A Chicken Coop

A bird was flying one day with a smaller bird in the grasp of it's claws which had fallen from her nest sight in mid-air, so she decided to give the young one a bird's eye view of the landscape near-by but was shot down over a near-by farm and the young one fell to the ground on the chicken yard.

Now the other chickens saw the whole thing, but the farmer didn't. So as he, while feeding them noticed it lying on the barn yard and put it in the coop because (His eye-sight was poor). Don't forget that statement.

Time past and every evening just before nightfall, all the chickens would head to the coop to roost, as in time the new bird grew larger, but the roosters steered clear of him, but the hens noticed nothing out of the ordinary. Months past and though the chickens were secure in their barn yard, one by one they came up missing with only their feathers, heads, wings and claws found. Even some of the roosters.

So the farmer then enclosed the TOP of the chicken coop to keep away other predators like coyotes, foxes, hawks, wolves, and owls or any other animals... yet the chickens still kept coming up MISSING.!

Confused now, he called in a specialist to see if he could find out what his problem was. But as he examined the coop, he discovered a unique difference in the look of one his chickens.

IT'S EYES "PIERCING", IT'S FEATHERS, "MASSIVE". IT'S BEAK, SHARP AND "POINTED DOWNWARD."! Then he said to the farmer whose vision was poor. You have a rare GOLDEN EAGLE….
"Stuck in A Chicken Coop!!! They are almost extinct and quite valuable and if you kill it, it can cost you the price of your farm.

The problems you are having, are the ones you created yourself. If you want to save your population of chickens, RELEASE IT AND SET IT FREE! See it, eating chickens is not it's first choice of food. It really likes RATS, SNAKES, and PRARIE DOGS and such as that. He eats meat. LET AN EAGLE…. BE AN EAGLE, but his first choice is to… CATCH FISH…. SET IT FREE, because Eagles eat chickens too.

This whole time this: BIRD OF PREY ate what you fed it without complaint. Hasn't anyone ever told you, you cannot feed Eagles; chicken feed? Or that THEY JUST KNOW WHAT AND WHO THEY REALLY ARE, and where you have placed them does not identify them…GOD DOES.

Sometimes, people label people the same way as chickens and place them in their small (cages of reason) because they have very poor vision and lack INSIGHT through their EYESIGHT and their perception of them because their points of reference are based only on things that they know about... and therefore, they (UNWITTINGLY LIMIT THEIR CEILINGS BECAUSE OF IT.) when what God meant for us is to be and will free us.

Once the owner of the cages began to see what God already knew about us when He made us and intended us to be, through the EYES of a specialist. His name is Jesus. Never let anyone convince you that you are...NOT WHO GOD SAYS YOU ARE, but wait ON THE LORD and in due season, He will set you free and you won't ever be permanently an "EAGLE"!... "Stuck in A Chicken Coop"! Exod.19:3-6,Is.40:28-31, Is.40:1-8.

I Had a Stunt-Double

A well-known actor who had just finished the last scene in a movie heard the director say: That's a wrap! We're done and everybody clapped their hands, shouted then went off to celebrate the shoot.

After editing sound, special effects and the film credits were added, the film that they had just finished shooting, WENT INTO PRODUCTION. To no one's surprise it was a blockbuster and the lead actor was not only nominated for an Oscar but a Golden Globe award also. So to promote the new release he had to go to many premieres and make special appearances and give interviews.

On one late-night talk show he was asked about his action scenes in the movie. How fluid and agile he was in the fight, car chases, acrobatics leaps and dives he did and yet he showed no signs that he had hardly broke sweat or was even out of breathe. The interviewer asked him: "You must be in tremendous shape to do all that stuff .He replied: "Not on your life not in the least bit"!! The people who hired me won't let me do any of that stuff because they say it's way too dangerous I could get hurt or even die trying.

"I Had A Stunt-Double". Somebody they pay just to make me look good! HE IS BUILT LIKE ME, WALKS LIKE ME, MOVES LIKE ME...but he is: NOT

ME.. and if you didn't know it, or I had let the secret out, you guys would have given me too much credit for work I didn't really do. I'm just giving credit to where credit is due. Somebody else had to do the real hard stuff, I just step in here when the <u>director</u> say: Cut! Then, he (the stunt- double) steps in.

Do you know we have a Stunt- Double? He is called an intercessor. Somebody who make us look like we did them...and makes us LOOK LIKE IT'S US. He doesn't however always get the credit He DESERVES yet the director allows Him to take my place ...all I have to do is: ......FOLLOW THE SCRIPT---URES ...(lol) Is.53:12 Ever pause the director gives, means it's time to PRAY. G.I.G.A.T.T.

The Hostage

A young child, about 10 years old stole some money from his father's wallet not knowing he was being watched in the process, was then confronted about it right after by his father who then asked: Michael? Did you take money from my wallet? And he responded back; "No daddy! I wouldn't do anything like that!! Now Michael had his hands behind his back as he talked back to him; so he asked him the same question again and got the same answer.

His father now furious knew he was lying said to him: Go to your room and don't come back 'til I say so. Pouting the child stormed off and shut the door. Days past and all he was allowed to do was go to school, do his homework, eat dinner, get a bath, then go back to his room all the while clinching the stolen money in his hand which he never spent.

Finally after about two weeks had passed without any change he finally asked his father to come to his room and talked with him. His father came and sat on the bed as the child angrily argued and complained about being "The Hostage" in this situation NOT being allowed to watch TV, play video games, talk on the phone or have his friends over, then finally admit he took his money, never spent it. Then said to his father: You made me: "The Hostage".

The father laughed and said to him: "Mike you were never the hostage son. Michael shockingly said: Dad that doesn't make any sense. I've been here all this time without privileges and you say I'm not: "The Hostage'? Then he said son: Truthfully the hostage is the TRUTH! YOU HAVE HELD THE TRUTH HOSTAGE! That's why you are…. (GET THIS) …. Not free!

See you held the truth in UNRIGHTEOUSNESS which make> YOU< the prisoner. The money you stole which you held behind your back was that truth!! "The Hostage". That is what you know is true and refuse to admit that it is. You then become the prisoner of lies and in constant denial and miserable, burdened with guilt. The more lies you tell and get away with, the more they numb your reality of the truth because the lies go without penalty but not without consequence.

It's only when you feel the penalty of the bondage of consequence which SEEMS like prison is when you feel that you are being made:" The Hostage." but one you created by lying in the first place. When you confess it, only then can you ever be free.

God like the movie is looking for: A Few Good Men. He constantly wants the TRUTH! When we are liberated but without penalty but without guilt. You want the truth? You want the truth? You Can't handle the truth! Or can you?

Freedom doesn't come by laws enacted, money exchanged or plea bargaining. It only comes because Jesus was: "The Hostage" who paid with His life so I could be free by admitting I am guilty. Jn.8:20-36, Rom.1:16-32, Jn.14:6, 1Jn.1:4-10.

<u>A Snake Under a Rock</u>

A man was cutting the grass on his lawn for the first time in the early spring. He had let it grow 'til it was nearly ankle-high and did so on purpose because he was trying to allow his newly planted grass seed to form a stronger root system so it would retain moisture on the hot summer days and stay greener longer.

But he had also had a rock garden where he had trees and plants growing in it also. So as he cut and edge it in order to give it the look he thought it deserved he had to remove some the larger Lava Rocks in the rock garden to weed-eat the few but noticeable weeds there.

And as he-----(bowed himself down in the garden), remember that phrase, beneath the rock there was: "A Snake Under a Rock." Startled at first, he moved away very quickly, 'til he evaluated the situation for a while. Then he began to laugh. See the snake was harmless and even if it were deadly, it was: Under A Rock! Had that rock not been moved, it would have never been discovered!

See the snake is in a ..... >>>>>.Good Place <<<<< Camouflaged, covered, feeding on frogs and lizards and going underground when it was threatened or evading a predator. He was no threat to it nor it to him. It taught him something about the Bible and how the scenario was in similar in this way.

The Snake was Judas. The Garden, of Gethsemane. The Rock, was Christ! Art was imitating life like a prayer in secret was being revealed in front of him.

Taking that lesson to heart showed that though there was pressure on Jesus in the garden it was nothing to the pressure that was being placed on Judas who killed himself from his own guilt.

If we bow in the garden of prayer the pressure is lifted off of us and then place on our enemies and they self-destruct all because of it and besides that, no snake can hurt us when stay far enough away knowing a snake is only as good as his range to strike us. One third it's body length.

It really doesn't matter. When we pray, we can laugh and say: AWH SHUCKS It's only "A Snake Under a Rock"! That rock is Jesus holding things down for us. BOO !!!!(lol)... SCARED YET? I THOUGHT NOT! Mrk.15:32-41, Mt.21:33-46, Ps.118:14-29, Acts.28:1-6 Mrk.16:14-20.

Explaining and Complaining

It never ceases to amaze me how something as simple as dialog can often turns into,a hostile confrontations when the resolves are simpler than either one of them who are having that confrontation have ever considering in the processed! Like two longtime friends of different ages, ethnicity, social economic backgrounds who nearly came to blows over a confidential conversation.

After being pulled apart and later cooling off, one observer who knew them both decided to try to help them get back into each other's good graces, he discovered they truly were the best of friends! Their differences came due to how each interpret what the other was saying. One was explaining and the other thought he was just complaining and had gotten tired of hearing him seemingly go on and on about his issues which varied, while the other was always trying to give solutions to the seeming problems.

Plain and simply neither really knew just how great the differences between them were. You see by his constant complaining and explaining it caused a misinterpretation it led to the argument, the lesson here is even simpler. Make sure even with close friends the ground work is laid out that the purpose for confiding is not always for an answer. Sometimes an explanation can be misunderstood as a complaint and when people think you complain too much and they can't give you the answer, then both of you end up totally unprepared for the consequences that follow. God in prayer always knows the difference in either case and is equipped to handle and resolve both whether we do both at the same time or singularly.He knows because He knows the difference and He is always ready the right solution.

And it's always easy to approach Him with what you're going through that is why prayer is such a great thing to practice with someone who knows the difference. Heb.4:12-16, Ps.42:1-8, Ps.34:1-19, Philip.4:6-13..!

Camouflage

I was studying wild-life. The Quails in particular, a mother quail with her brood scuttles them through the woods always watching out for predators like owls, coyotes, foxes, hawks, and snakes. Being sought after by so many other creatures you would think and wonder: How do they survive?

It's almost a no-brainer really! "Camouflage." They know how to cloak themselves and blended into sometimes dense environment like thorny brush, leaf litter, and dirt, and rocks so they either are able to go un-noticed, overlooked and or too difficult to be sought after.

Kind of like going to the altar in prayer. Life has a way of pursuing us but if we learn from the quail how easy it is just to survive. The secret? To be looked OUT FOR BY someone who knows the environment. Secondly, find and adapt to what is around you, be still and KNOW you are safe 'til danger passes. Then GO ON WITH YOUR LIFE!...AT THE CROSS !!!! Ps.27:4-8, Hidden in PLAIN SIGHT. See a pavilion is open air and for observation. You can see what coming your way and yet you're out of reach at the same time.

Looking out and yet untouched unharmed unnoticed right before your eyes yet covered by the blood of Christ: in "Camouflage". Ps.46:10,. Ps. 23.

<u>You Still Got It</u>

Being a singer whose history of doing so goes back to my child hood, I am occasionally asked more often than not, to sing a song from back in tha' day. You know the songs. The ones that made you feel good or reminded you of an old flame or a good time, which when I am asked to do so, I try to accommodate who ever ask me to by singing a few bars or a verse or two just to have fun and most of the time I get this response: "You Still Got It" D-Mo.

I am flattered to hear that. It lets me know that though I've changed, my voice has not ...at least not that much (AS FAR AS THEY CAN TELL) though I know better. Better or the same could apply to anyone about their looks, style, weight, height, etc. and some have even gotten better in all areas of their lives contrary to how time has changed things around them.

I saw a guy at the gym who now is much much older and was asked by the newcomers who remembered him when they first came there, could he bench 250 lbs. He did.... Only to hear them then say: man, "You Still Got It".

The phrase implies that SOME THINGS ABOUT US HAVE NOT CHANGED. Hopefully those are Good Things. What it further implies is that we can carry on some behavioral patterns long after they were thought to have diminished.

The point I'm getting at is this: If we met God face to face or ask Him through the vehicle of Prayer, does He still walk on water, raise the dead, feed the hungry, heal the sick or still do miracles all because we can't find current evidence to support if we tested Him to see if He Still has it! Here's how we would know for sure.

We should ask Him ourselves not as a test, but as a RESOLVE. Out of a need to prove He is God rather than just impress us. We do that through need, not to flatter ourselves by His efforts or try to flatter or BE flattered by Him.

Jesus welcomes that kind of challenge because once He does show himself as Lord. Our testimony tells others in the form as a witness, when we glorify Him with praise by telling others what He's done for us. Leaving them miffed at His Power and seeking Him themselves for His miracles works so that they say about Him to ask Him themselves then pursue Him as their answer, they THEN shout His Praise in Worship saying: Jesus!:"You Still Got It."! Jn.20:19-28, Heb.13:8-15, Mal.3:1-7, Jas.1:16& 17, Ps.37:23-26.

The Path of Least Resistance

Water.! The most useful and necessary liquid on the planet. Even science, when exploring the universe, make a declaration that in searching for life elsewhere in space that ALL LIVING THINGS, HAS TO HAVE IT in order to survive, (PERIOD!)

Yet there is a strange dichotomy about water. That is it's innate ability to almost always take "The Path Of Least Resistance" over land, crevasses, levees, landscapes, as if it is weak, but the dichotomy is a deception.

People have drowned in only a few inches of it. It has <u>swept away whole cities alone because the FORCE of</u> water is more powerful than most people can even imagine.

Sometimes even some people are said to appear to be as weak as water when they sometimes take a path that in some ways appear as PASSIVE, OR NON-VIOLENT, but if they believe in God, THEY ARE AS WATER. DECEPTIVE in this regard.

When they pray, they muster up forces that can move mountains, sweep away enemies, shallow up problems and overcome obstacles in their way. Simply by calling upon the Name of The Lord the Bible says: The Lord Is a Strong Tower. The Righteous Run (TO IT) and are safe.

So rather than appearing strong up against your problems to overcome them, try: "The Path of Least Resistance"! Flood the altar with your tears. They in turn will open the flood-gates of Heaven and rain down blessings in your favor and trouble for: "The Path of Least Resistance" is on our knees, but the Force of that path, clears away all ADVSERSITY! Jn.4:10-14, Mt.5:36-46, Mt.17:13-20, Ps.110:1-7, Prov.18:10, Ps.46. "The Path of Least Resistance"!

Manipulation

It never ceases to amaze me how some people feel it's their duty to dictate policy for other people's lives when secretly it only works to their advantage to do so. They with all use their wit and wisdom feeling that those they do that to are naïve and don't know how to lead their own lives and must be steered in the direction the will help them accomplish their goals, when in truth, they are only using them inadvertently with the tool of: "Manipulation".

They've never given much thought to who's life they are changing and why they selfishly want things IN THOSE LIVES to go as they want them to. Personal ambition is the real culprit behind their need to change others. Ambition can be detached, merciless, consumed in it's desire to reach its's own goals, objective even at the expense of the lack of understanding or compassion or the Golden Rule: As you would that men do unto you, do ye unto them.

God's only calling on us is for us to be saved and love one another. He never forces or coerces us. Man is the only creature in creation that has complete and total FREE WILL yet we are sometimes bent on controlling the lives and well-being of our fellows brothers and sister.

See "Manipulation" has a partner. His name is Power! When we become power crazed, we also become control freaks and yet get indignant when we are met with change or a challenge brought on by someone else as they demand the same from us!

How do we fix it? First we must accept the differences in, of, and with other people and learn from them, that is called understanding. Then and only then we kill "Manipulation".

We acquire this trait through our prayer life. Talking to God in prayer causes us to read His word and learn HIS DISPOSITION...on a personal level because we also learn the difference between "Manipulation" and Discipleship...a free will self-disciplined through the virtue of love.

Love is a quality that command respect without demanding it...thus eliminate the need to make things work to our advantage in the lives of others yet it changes them through the example it presents as it is represented in our respect for them, there by changing them will-fully.

It covers a multitude of faults and creates growth That is what Jesus taught and manipulates our praise voluntarily.

Want to change the world? Be changed through your talk with God....and change around you will be done without any external influences on our part. God intended it that way...Changed affecting change the perfected formula for : " Manipulation".

1kgs.6:11-20,Js.5:13-18,Mt.5:13-16, Jn.14:19-27,Jn.13:34&35.

12 Years A Slave

Art imitates life in so many ways and we miss it's other meanings sometimes. Here let me quickly show you with a movie: 12 Years A Slave. For those who never saw it, it has to do with a free black man who got drugged and ended up a slave. A slave master who took his papers, chained him, stole him from his surroundings and worked him in a harsh plantation environment far away from his home and family. All the while KNOWING HE WAS A FREE MAN.

After 12 years and attempt by letter and on foot he sought his freedom anew until he was finally discovered by representatives of his state who took him away from that cruel slave master and sent back home to his family all the while keeping a diary of the whole ordeal. Thank God for vindication but unbeknownst to us, we can be just like that slave master in every way.

We see God forgive people after they confess a hope in his salvation and redemption but are sometimes willingly and woefully UNWILLING TO LET THEM GO ON WITH THEIR LIVES ...FREE. AS IF THEIR FREEDOM DEPENDS ON US. We seduce them , entrap them, chain them and even TRY TO make them pay harsh penalties because ...WE CAN NOT FORGIVE (WHAT IS NOT EVEN OUR'S TO FORGIVE..THEIR SINS BEFORE GOD HIMSELF AND GIVE THEM THEIR RESTORATION. As if we are to determine whose good enough, clean enough, righteous enough, so we imprison them as slave labor BY CONSTANTLY reminding them BY BRINGING UP THEIR PAST because we cannot or will not except their forgiveness as equal to our own and BEING THE SAME.

We then quote God's word as the standard using people like Moses, David, Abraham, Jacob, Solomon, Jonah, Job, Paul, or Peter just to name a few we honor them (we honor them) with memory loss and say we in this regard forgetting their past indiscretions as we honor them as holy men.

So let me talk about those guys a second. Moses was a murderer. David an adulterer. Abraham a liar. Jacob a deceiver and trickster. Solomon a polygamist and an idolater. Jonah was disobedient. Job self-righteous. Paul, a Bounty hunter and gang banger and Peter a coward yet we honor them as Godly. When people we know personally we categorize as sub-standard with the SAME character flaws as they had yet we think that they don't measure up to what we think God's true standards are and are no different than the afore mentioned.

Forgiven by God through Christ yet we quote those names mentioned in the Bible shamelessly as we judge and enslave our brothers and sisters with their past and we broadcast their past deeds every chance we somehow thinking we are not at all like them being : "Twelve Years A Slave" on our plantations of un-forgiveness .

How hypocritical we are unwittingly all because we can't let go of (THEIR PAST) thinking of it differently from our own or even those written in the Bible itself accounted worthy, when Jesus died for all who repent THROUGH PRAYER so any one forgiven by Him can be in Heaven and NOT "Twelve Years A Slave."

Jn.8:1-36...Rom.10:1-13...Is.61:1-7....Lk.15:17-32..1 Jn.1:4-10....

Rev. Don W. Moses

About The Author

Don W. Moses is the sixth of nine children born to Bishop and Tracie V. Moses of North Little Rock, Arkansas. He grew up during the segregation, civil rights and Viet Nam eras and attended public school in North Little Rock, Arkansas. He graduated from S.A. Jones High School in North Little Rock, Arkansas in 1968.

While in High School, Don lettered in Basketball and Track High Jump Competitions. Upon graduation, Don received a 4 year full Music Scholarship to Langston University in Langston, OK, He chose a military career instead and served in the U.S. Navy until 1970. Upon his return fro the Navy, Don worked for Kroger Co. and sang with a local band called the Lyrics and the Playboys.

In 1971, Don was called to the Ministry at 8th Street Baptist Church at the age of 22. Currently he serves as the Associate Minister at the Morning Star Baptist Church where Robert Jenkins is the Pastor. He is an active Choir member, serves as a teacher in Union District of Christian Education wherein he also serves as Co-Youth Director with his wife Linda(Evans) Moses. His mission is to serve in community outreach ministry which assists with the sick and shut-in and the hospital ministry.

Don is also a devoted participant in the National Baptist Convention

Don recently retired after serving 39 years as a Locomotive Engineer with Union Pacific Railroad. During a 40 year period following his entry into the ministry, Don developed several hobbies which includes, sports, fishing, singing and writing poems and short stories. As he explored his hobby of writing, he realized that God has transferred spiritual life messages and lessons to be shared. It was these revelation that led him to write for several decades a series of Poems and Epiphanies that reveal understandings to the ordinary lay persons about the power and presence of God in the most "ordinary" experiences. And is currently an associate at The Morning Star Baptist Church

The Epiphanies of Prayer Book is Reverend Moses's second book. His first book, The Play of Words: A Poets Know, was published in 2017.